PAUL G. KAUPER

THE HIGHER LAW AND THE RIGHTS OF MAN IN A REVOLUTIONARY SOCIETY

Distinguished Lecture Series
on
the Bicentennial

revolution · continuity · promise

PAUL G. KAUPER

THE HIGHER LAW AND THE RIGHTS OF MAN IN A REVOLUTIONARY SOCIETY

Delivered at
Old North Church, Boston, Massachusetts
on November 7, 1973

American Enterprise Institute for Public Policy Research
Washington, D. C.

© 1974 by American Enterprise Institute
for Public Policy Research, Washington, D. C.

ISBN 0-8447-1302-3

Library of Congress Catalog Card Number L.C. 74-76424

Printed in the United States of America

The American Revolution was both radical and conservative. It asserted the right of people to revolt against established authority. It declared that government derives its authority from popular consent. Its central document proclaimed the radical idea that all men are created equal.

But the Revolution had its conservative overtones. It found its intellectual justification in ideas and principles with long established historical foundations. It had its roots in English legal and political institutions and in a body of thought—theological, moral and philosophic—which had universal dimensions. Old and essentially conservative ideas and traditions were harnessed to the cause of revolution. In turn they laid the foundation for a new constitutionalism which has survived because it has a capacity for change and yet remains loyal to the ancient truths that have given continuity to the system.

It was no accident that men trained in law played prominent roles in the revolutionary struggle and the subsequent transformation from a confederation to a federal union. Constitutional thinking was a key support in the intellectual structure which undergirded the American Revolution. Central to this thinking was the concept of the "higher law," to which ultimate recourse could be made in judging the validity of ordinary enactments. Two principal components merged to shape this concept. One was the idea of natural law and the corollary idea of natural rights. The other was the tradition of the English common law as embodying a system of justice founded on right and reason. Natural law

1

and natural right on the one hand, and the view of the common law as basic and fundamental law on the other, were twin notions that fitted together naturally to produce the idea of "higher law" that emerged as a powerful force not only in supporting the claim of the colonists but in laying the foundation of the American constitutional system.[1]

I

The idea of a natural law that is transcendent, that has divine sanction, that epitomizes wisdom, truth and morality, and to which positive law is subject had its origins in classical antiquity. During the Middle Ages natural law found its classical theological exposition in the *Summa* of St. Thomas Aquinas, which was the basis of the Church's juridical and political thinking and which came to be identified with large claims of ecclesiastical authority. Later came the writings of Puffendorf, Grotius, Vattel and others which upheld the law of nature in laying the foundation for the law of nations. The Enlightenment gave new impetus to natural law thinking in the Western world and particularly in England from where in turn it influenced the American colonies. The natural law of the Enlightenment, while essentially humanistic and not to be identified with the natural law of the Church, which rests on revelation, nevertheless carried the imprimatur of deistic thinking. But it

---

[1] On this point, see Edward S. Corwin, *The "Higher Law" Background of American Constitutional Law* (Ithaca, N.Y.: Cornell University Press, 1955).

For a survey of the lineage of natural law and natural rights thinking, see John C. H. Wu, *Fountain of Justice: A Study in the Natural Law* (New York: Sheed and Ward, 1955). For concise treatments, see Corwin, *The "Higher Law" Background of American Constitutional Law,* and M. Cappelletti, *Judicial Review in the Contemporary World* (Indianapolis: Bobbs-Merrill Co., 1971), pp. 25-43.

On natural rights generally, see C. J. Antieau, *Rights of Our Fathers* (Coiner, Virginia: Vienna Publications, 1968), and "Natural Rights and the Founding Fathers—The Virginians," *Washington and Lee Law Review,* vol. 17 (1960), p. 43; J. Maritain, *The Rights of Man and Natural Law* (London: The Centenary Press, 1944); J. C. Murray, *The Problem of Religious Freedom* (Westminster, Maryland: The Newman Press, 1965).

was John Locke, in his *Second Treatise on Civil Government,* who perhaps more than any other single person articulated the ideas of natural law that were influential in shaping American constitutional thinking.

Equally influential was the coupling of natural law with the idea of natural rights. The view that man is a creature of God, reflects the divine wisdom, enjoys the liberty to use his natural faculties and may assert a freedom against the arbitrary exercise of authority was a natural corollary of a transcendent law of reason that emphasized truth and morality. These rights were not created by law but were recognized and sanctioned by it: they were antecedent to positive law, and the law's function was to preserve and protect them.

This idea of natural rights was a basic ingredient in the thinking of the American colonists. Speaking for the Supreme Court in 1963, Mr. Justice Clark said: "the fact that the Founding Fathers believed devotedly that there was a God and that the unalienable rights of man were rooted in Him is clearly evidenced in their writings, from the Mayflower Compact to the Constitution itself." [2] The writings and speeches of the Founding Fathers abounded in expressions of the idea that men enjoyed basic freedoms which were the gift of God and were therefore immutable and unalienable. James Otis, defending the rights of the colonists, said that if the charter privileges of the colonists were disregarded or revoked, there still remained "the natural, inherent, and inseparable rights of men and citizens." [3] John Adams spoke of "rights antecedent to all earthly government, rights that cannot be repealed or restrained by human laws—rights derived from the great Legislator of the universe." [4] In a writing which preceded the Declaration of Independence, Jefferson asserted that "The God who gave life gave us liberty at the same time." [5] He also said that

---

[2] School District of Abington Township v. Schempp, 374 U.S. 203 at 213 (1963).

[3] J. Otis, *The Rights of the British Colonies Asserted and Proved* (pamphlet privately printed in Boston, 1764), quoted in Adams, *Life and Works* (Boston: Little, Brown and Company 1850-56), vol. 10, p. 293.

[4] John Adams, *Life and Works,* vol. 3, pp. 448-464.

[5] Thomas Jefferson, "Summary View," in *Papers,* ed. J. P. Boyd (Princeton: Princeton University Press, 1950), vol. 1, p. 135.

"our right to life, liberty, the use of our faculties, the pursuit of happiness is not left to the feeble and sophistical investigations of reason, but is impressed on the sense of every man. We do not claim these under the charter of kings or legislators, but under the King of kings." [6] George Mason identified natural rights as "the sacred rights of human nature." [7] Writing in 1774, Alexander Hamilton declared: "the sacred rights of mankind . . . are written, as with a sunbeam, in the whole volume of human nature, by the hand of the divinity itself, and can never be erased or obscured by mortal power." [8] Indeed, it is fair to say that, for the Founding Fathers, it was the idea of natural rights rather than rights developed at the common law which furnished the undergirding for the revolutionary movement.[9] King and Parliament had violated these rights and therefore the colonists were morally justified in asserting their independence.

These ideas found their classical expression at Jefferson's hands in the great language of the Declaration of Independence:

> When in the course of human events, it becomes necessary for one people to dissolve the political bands which have connected them with another, and to assume among the powers of the earth, the separate and equal station to which the laws of nature and of nature's God entitle them, a decent respect to the opinions of mankind requires that they should declare the causes which impel them to the separation.
>
> We hold these truths to be self-evident, that all men are created equal, that they are endowed by their Creator with certain unalienable rights, that among these are life, liberty and the pursuit of happiness. . . .

The document speaks of "the law of nature and of nature's God," says that "all men are created equal" and are endowed by

[6] Thomas Jefferson, *Works,* ed. Ford (New York and London: G. P. Putnam's Sons, 1904-05) , p. 66.

[7] Helen Hill, *George Mason, Constitutionalist* (Cambridge, Mass.: Harvard University Press, 1938) , p. 249.

[8]Alexander Hamilton, *Works,* ed. Henry C. Lodge (New York and London: G. P. Putnam's Sons, 1885-86) , vol. 1, p. 108.

[9] Antieau, *Rights of Our Fathers,* pp. 191-192.

their Creator with "unalienable rights." Jefferson's preference for the phrase "the law of nature and of nature's God," rather than for "natural law," is a characteristic expression of deistic thinking. It is significant that he invokes an ultimate divine source of moral law and of natural rights. The appeal is to the divine law that governs men and their institutions and that is the source of the equality of men and of the rights which belong to them as creatures of God. This was the foundation for the Declaration's reasoned discourse on the grievances of the colonists and on their right to declare their independence of English rule. Resting its case on natural law and natural rights, the Declaration remains an abiding affirmation of the higher law to which men and their governments are subject.

A further line of natural law thought entering into the main stream of American constitutionalism is found in the theological and political contributions that stemmed from the Protestant Reformation and were given their most effective expression by the Puritans and Presbyterians. The idea of the two kingdoms (both under God), the necessity for law as a restraint on evil and on the abuse of power, the idea of civic righteousness, the combination of individualism and social conscience, the emphasis on the charter as basic law, the notion of limited power, and the commitment to democracy and majority rule helped shape not only the concept but also the substance of the higher law. They provided justification for revolt against established authority, and furnished an important strand of thought for the fabric of American constitutionalism.[10]

The contribution of common law tradition to the idea of higher law was equally impressive. The intellectual leaders of the colonies well understood the rights of Englishmen as they had been hammered out on the anvil of experience. Lawyers had been nurtured in Blackstone. They were well versed in John Locke. James Otis, in denouncing the infamous writs of assistance, demonstrated his intimacy with the English precedents that supported the freedom from unreasonable search and seizure. More impor-

---

[10] See P. Miller, *Errand Into the Wilderness* (Cambridge, Mass: The Belknap Press of Harvard University, 1956), pp. 142-150; also Corwin *The "Higher Law" Background of American Constitutional Law*, pp. 61-77.

tant, however, than the specific contents of the common law and the rights that grew within its protection was the process and authority it claimed. A system hammered out on the anvil of pragmatic experience, embodying the rule of reason, relying on precedent for its development, and fortified by documents (beginning with Magna Carta) that resulted from constitutional crises and attested the rights of Englishmen, it acquired at the hand of lawyers and judges a concreteness and toughness which inspired respect, commanded authority, and gave direction to English constitutional development. Most important, in elevating the role of reason and emphasizing the central role of the judges, it became a symbol of a fundamental law that achieved justice, articulated and protected the rights of Englishmen, and served as a limitation against abuse of power. For Englishmen it epitomized the rule of law. Rulers were subject to it. Bracton had said that the king was "under God and under the law." [11] Sir Edward Coke, the pre-eminent prophet of the common law who had led the fight against the Crown, who went back to Magna Carta for his inspiration, and who was a champion of English right, found "common right and reason" to be the genius of English law and liberties. Indeed, Coke declared that "when an Act of Parliament is against common right or reason . . . the common law will control it and adjudge such Act to be void." [12] Thus common law became identified with a higher law, and a powerful tool was forged for asserting the supremacy of the law and the role of the judges in interpreting and applying it.

Great documents produced in time of crisis have added strength to the common law tradition. Out of Magna Carta, wrested by the barons from King John, had come the idea that men could not be deprived of life, liberty, or property except in accordance with the law of the land—an idea which later found expression in the notion of due process of law, an enduring English contribution to constitutional thinking. The Petition of Right

---

[11] Henry Bracton, *Bracton on the Laws and Customs of England,* Samuel Thorne and George Woodbine, eds. (Cambridge, Mass.: The Belknap Press of Harvard University, 1968), vol. 2, p. 33; original title: *De Legibus et Consuetudinibus Angliae.*

[12] Dr. Bonham's Case, 8 Coke 118a (1610).

(1628) and the Bill of Rights (1689) affirmed the basic rights of Englishmen. The written document, a symbol and a beacon to which men could appeal in later generations, assumed its place in the higher law tradition. Following in this great tradition, the colonists also looked to a written document wherein they publicly proclaimed their rights and gave a reasoned statement in support of the decision to assert their right to self-government.

Acceptance of natural law and natural rights, coupled with reverence for the common law as itself embodying the law of reason and for historic documents declaring right, combined powerfully to establish the "higher law" thinking which permeated the Revolution and laid the foundation for a remarkable constitutional development. Indeed, American constitutional history, the crises it has witnessed, and the development which has ensued can be viewed as an explication of the higher law.

The constitutions adopted by the individual states incorporated ideas that were a distillate of the experience and reasoning implicit in the natural law and its processes: the people as the source of power, the right of self-determination, the right of the people to vote and to participate in the government through their elected representatives, the rule of law, the charter as a limitation on power, the separation of powers as a means of checking abuse of authority, the inherent rights of the citizen, and the role of the independent judiciary in protecting the citizens and asserting the supremacy of the law.[13] Underlying it all was the central notion that government derived its authority from the people and was subject therefore to limitations imposed and liberties reserved. The new state constitutions contained "declarations of right." The use of the word "declarations" warrants emphasis. The constitutions did not create these rights; rather they declared rights that were derived from what was stated in the Declaration of Independence to be the self-evident truth—that all men are endowed by their Creator with certain unalienable rights including the right to life, liberty, and the pursuit of happiness.

The adoption of state constitutions preceded the adoption and ratification of the federal Constitution drafted at Philadelphia in

---

[13] For texts of the early state constitutions, see R. L. Perry and J. C. Cooper, *Sources of Our Liberties* (Chicago: American Bar Foundation, 1959).

1787. Unlike the Declaration, which was a political document, the Constitution was a carefully drafted legal document. Resting on the authority of the people and premised on republican principles of government, the Constitution defined and allocated authority. Its carefully devised system of checks and balances, implementing the separation of powers, was premised on the assumption, as Madison noted, that men are not angels, that the grant of power invites abuse, and that restraints are necessary to curb its exercise.[14] Those limitations on power epitomized the rule of law. When faithfully enforced by an independent judiciary, they constitute the bulwark for protection of the liberties of the citizen.

Noticeably absent in the Constitution, however, was a declaration of rights. We need not rehearse all of the historical factors leading to this omission except to note that those who played a leading role in the drafting thought a bill of rights unnecessary because they did not find it conceivable that the scope of the federal powers would permit an intrusion into the rights reserved to the people or to the states. This view, however, did not go unchallenged. To meet the challenge, the first ten articles of amendment, commonly known as the Bill of Rights, were adopted shortly after the Constitution itself went into effect. Specific rights are guaranteed in the first eight amendments. The great freedoms are there—beginning with freedom of religion, speech, press and assembly, and petition for the redress of grievances. But significantly the Ninth Amendment declared that the enumeration of these privileges and rights should not be construed to deny or disparage others retained by the people. This was a clear expression that the rights set forth in the Bill of Rights were not created by the Bill of Rights but were simply declared there. The Ninth Amendment implicitly embodies natural rights philosophy.

Thus the stage was set for the great American experiment in government under a written charter. Two great principles of that government received their classic exposition by John Marshall in his opinion in *Marbury* v. *Madison*: the Constitution is the funda-

---

[14] *The Federalist,* number 51 (Everman's Library Edition, 1911), p. 264. Charles Beard ascribed this paper to Madison; see Charles A. Beard, *The Enduring Federalist* (Garden City: Doubleday & Co., 1948), p. 210.

mental law of the land, and it is distinctively the function of the judiciary to give this law its authoritative interpretation. These two principles of paramount law and the judicial function in interpreting this law are unique aspects of American constitutional development. Their relationship to the theory of natural law and natural right is readily apparent. Once the people have reduced their thinking on the fundamental structure of government and on their reserved rights into a written document, the ideas of natural law and natural rights tend to merge into this document. The document then becomes the symbol of the higher law of the land. The veneration popularly accorded the Constitution amply demonstrates this tendency in the popular mind. The higher law acquires concreteness through a process whereby an independent judicial tribunal interprets the law in a final and authoritative way so that natural law and natural rights are happily absorbed into positive law through the process of empiric adjudication. Indeed, for some, the Constitution thereby acquires even a divine sanction.

Care must be taken, however, in identifying the Constitution with a transcendent natural law and the Bill of Rights with natural rights. Basic principles expressed in a constitution can certainly be identified with a body of universal and enduring ideas that reflect reasoned conclusions on human nature, the function of government, and the institutions designed to channel and limit power. But the particular institutional arrangements worked out at the Philadelphia convention, as a response to immediate historical experience and in a number of instances as a compromise of opposing ideas, should not be viewed as the ultimate expression of these principles. Indeed, the framers, while hoping to establish "a constitution intended to endure for ages to come and consequently to be adapted to the various crises of human affairs," [15] recognized that specific institutional arrangements might be transient when they provided a mechanism for amending the Constitution.

An even more important consideration is that natural law, however conceived and whatever its authority, must necessarily

---

[15] John Marshall, in McCulloch v. Maryland, 17 U.S. (4 Wheat.) 316, at 415 (1819).

remain outside the Constitution and not be confused with it. Ultimate values, goals to be achieved, principles relevant to new movements in national life, ideas of freedom, right, justice, and morality have their inception in theological, philosophical, moral, and social thinking which transcends the Constitution. The validity of any constitution may be judged by recourse to the higher law.

One constitutional scholar has observed that the natural rights on which there was the largest measure of agreement among the Virginians were freedom of conscience, freedom of communication, the right to be free from arbitrary laws, the rights of assembly and petition, the property right, and the right of self-government.[16] To these may be added equality in the enjoyment of right. These were rights inherent in the idea of man as a moral and rational creature entitled to the full enjoyment of his faculties. Not all of these rights were expressly captured in the Bill of Rights. On the other hand, some rights receiving positive recognition, such as the right to trial by jury, can hardly be called natural rights. They are ancillary rights that help to protect natural rights.[17]

That there was still a natural law outside the Constitution was made manifest in the great struggle over the slavery issue. Jefferson had boldly declared in the Declaration of Independence that all men are created equal and that this is self-evident, as are those unalienable rights with which all men are endowed. It became painfully evident that this grand assertion could not be reconciled with an institution whereby one race held another in subjection for forced labor.[18] In the sharp and bitter struggles over the question of extending the institution of slavery to new territories and over the abolitionists' demands that all slavery be abolished, slavery emerged as the nation's great moral issue.

The abolitionists could point to the Declaration of Independence as stating a self-evident natural right on the part of all men to freedom and to equal treatment. The Constitution itself had

---

[16] Antieau, "Natural Rights and the Founding Fathers—The Virginians," pp. 45-46.

[17] Antieau, *Rights of Our Fathers,* pp. 103-104.

[18] See M. D. Howe, "Federalism and Civil Rights," in Cox, Howe and Wiggins, *Civil Rights, the Constitution and the Courts* (Cambridge, Mass.: Harvard University Press, 1967), pp. 30-55.

made a nodding concession to the slavery problem in permitting the termination of the slave trade after 1808 and in fixing the formula for apportioning seats in Congress; but it also imposed a duty to return runaway slaves to owners. Moreover, in the celebrated Dred Scott decision of 1857, the Supreme Court went so far as to say that the slave-owner had a constitutionally protected property interest in his slaves, so that for the law to deprive him of that interest when he took a slave into free territory was itself a deprivation of property without due process of law. But a judicial decision that rested on considerations incompatible with basic moral concepts could not in the end command respect. Abraham Lincoln said that the Dred Scott decision was morally wrong and should be changed. William Seward, in his sharp criticism of the Court, declared that there is a higher law than the Constitution. In fact, the issue of slavery, unsolvable by judicial or political means, required four years of bloody conflict for its resolution.

Out of the Civil War came a radically revised constitutional order and an extraordinary increase in those rights accorded federal protection. The Thirteenth, Fourteenth, and Fifteenth Amendments were designed to give constitutional status and protection to the former black slaves and rested on the idea of human equality that the Declaration had declared to be a natural right. Viewed from the perspective of general constitutional theory, the Fourteenth Amendment had the widest and most pervasive significance. The provision that no state should deprive any person of life, liberty or property without due process of law or deny to any person the equal protection of the laws defined ideas of rights which were readily identifiable with natural rights. The Fourteenth Amendment marked a revolution in the protection of rights and led to what we may call the nationalization of right. In the hands of the judiciary, it became a tool for implementing the grand assertion of the Declaration of Independence that all men should have equal opportunities to enjoy life, liberty, and the pursuit of happiness.

Notwithstanding a very modest beginning in its interpretation of the Fourteenth Amendment, the Supreme Court eventually embarked upon a use of the due process clause which made it into an extraordinary tool for reviewing state laws that might impair what the Court came to call fundamental rights protected under the rubrics of life, liberty and property. In the process the Court formulated the "fundamental rights" interpretation of due process.[19] Although it never succeeded in arriving at a particularly illuminating definition of fundamental rights, it did try in various ways to define them. They were the rights that "are of the very essence of a scheme of ordered liberty," [20] that are founded in "those fundamental principles of liberty and justice which lie at the base of all our civil and political institutions," [21] that are "rooted in the traditions and conscience of our people," [22] that are "essential to the orderly pursuit of happiness by free men." [23] Simply to repeat these phrases is to make clear that the judicial conception of fundamental rights draws its inspiration from natural rights tradition.[24]

For a period of about fifty years the Court employed the due process clause chiefly as a vehicle for invalidating legislation found to infringe arbitrarily upon economic rights such as the freedom of contract and the use of property. But the experience in this period, despite the perversion of natural rights thinking to serve ends inimical to legitimate public interests, had an enduring value because of the Court's identification of the due process clause with

---

[19] For a brief review of this development, see Kauper, "Penumbras, Peripheries, Emanations, Things Fundamental and Things Forgotten: The Griswold Case," *Michigan Law Review,* vol. 64 (1965), p. 235.

[20] Palko v. Connecticut, 302 U.S. 319 at 325 (1937).

[21] Hebert v. Louisiana, 277 U.S. 312 at 312 (1926).

[22] Snyder v. Massachusetts, 291 U.S. 97 at 105 (1934).

[23] Meyer v. Nebraska, 262 U.S. 390 at 399 (1923).

[24] In his dissenting opinion in the Slaughterhouse Cases, 83 U.S. (16 Wallace) 36 at 105 (1873), Justice Field declared that the Fourteenth Amendment was intended "to give practical effect to the declaration of 1776 of inalienable rights, rights which are the gift of the Creator, which the law does not confer but only recognizes."

fundamental rights and because of its insistence that arbitrary or unreasonable restrictions on these rights resulted in a deprivation without due process of law.[25] During the New Deal the Court abandoned this emphasis upon economic liberty as a fundamental right and turned its attention toward the protection of the individual against arbitrary procedures and the protection of personal and societal freedoms, including the freedom of speech, press, assembly and religion.[26]

A great controversy within the Court has turned on the question of whether the due process clause should be interpreted to incorporate within its protection, as a limitation on the power of the states, the specific guarantees of the first eight amendments originally designated as restrictions on the federal government only. Some members of the Court held that fundamental rights were not necessarily those identified in the Bill of Rights but only those of a very basic character, more akin to natural rights.[27] Other justices, Mr. Justice Black among them, argued that the Bill of Rights set forth the ultimate wisdom of the Declaration of Rights and that any recognition of fundamental rights must at least begin with the first eight amendments, and perhaps even be limited to them. In a notable dissenting opinion, Mr. Justice Black attacked the fundamental rights interpretation of the due process clause as it had evolved historically in the Court's decisions. First, he said that the Fourteenth Amendment's original purpose was to make the Bill of Rights apply to the states. Second, he contended that the Court's use of the fundamental rights theory

---

[25] It is worth noting that during this same period, the Court invalidated state laws which prohibited the teaching in public schools in any language other than the English language, Meyer v. Nebraska, 262 U.S. 390 (1922); which required parents to send their children to public schools, Pierce v. Society of Sisters, 268 U.S. 510 (1925); which unduly restricted freedom of the press, Near v. Minnesota 283 U.S. 697 (1931); and which violated freedom of assembly, De Jonge v. Oregon, 299 U.S. 353 (1937). It also laid the foundation for the fairness doctrine in applying the due process clause to protect the accused. See Moore v. Dempsey, 261 U.S. 86 (1923).

[26] For a review, see Kauper, *Frontiers of Constitutional Liberty* (Ann Arbor, Mich.: University of Michigan Law School, 1956), p. 21 et seq.

[27] For a review, see Justice Cardozo's opinion in Palko v. Connecticut, 302 U.S. 319 (1937), and Justice Frankfurter's concurring opinion in Adamson v. California, 332 U.S. 46 at 59 (1947).

was premised upon an application of the idea of natural law, an idea which he characterized as "an incongruous excrescence on our Constitution." [28]

This latter observation is worth particular attention. It is evident that Justice Black was a positivist in his jurisprudential thinking and that his remark reflected the general decline of natural law and natural rights thinking in America. This decline can be traced to the rise of science and secular humanism in the latter part of the nineteenth century. The idea of a transcendent natural or moral law then fell into disrepute. With this began the era of positivism in American jurisprudence, well epitomized in the writing and opinions of Mr. Justice Holmes. In the eyes of the positivist, law is viewed in historical and humanistic terms. To put it in constitutional terms, rights are significant only as they find concrete expression in the historic document. There are no rights outside the Constitution, and the business of the law is simply to develop concrete solutions to concrete problems based on the application of the text as informed by history and reason.

Justice Black's picture of natural law in his dissent in the *Adamson* case was particularly unfortunate because it disregarded the honored place that natural law thinking had had in the early days of the republic and had long enjoyed in the American legal tradition. To label natural law "an excrescence on our Constitution" was to be particularly insensitive to a significant part of American constitutional development.

Justice Black led a movement within the Court to divorce the Court's interpretation of due process from the idea that there were fundamental rights not identified in the Bill of Rights. For the most part he was successful—at least in his insistence that the express guarantees of the first eight amendments should be recognized as fundamental rights. But it is illusory to suppose that, even so, the Court has abandoned natural rights thinking. An examination of its opinions shows that the result is rarely dictated by the explicit language of the text. Rather it stems from a reasoned interpretation illuminated but not controlled by history and in-

---

[28] See Justice Black's dissent in Adamson v. California, 332 U.S. 46 at 68 et seq. (1947).

14

spired by an understanding of ultimate values which are at most implicit in the constitutional order.

Examination of the Court's decisions in recent years makes it clear that the values of a democratic society have emerged as most important—religious liberty and freedom of conscience, the basic freedoms of expression, the rights attached to self-government and the citizen's participation in it, the protection of the individual against arbitrary restraint, his freedom to pursue his own way and cultivate his faculties, and the protection of minorities against invidious discrimination. These are readily equated with natural right categories. The emphasis on these aspects of liberty represents a choice of values by the Supreme Court, values which turn on the worth and dignity of the person and on the institutions and procedures that are unique to a democratic society. We come back, then, to what perhaps is the most fundamental aspect of natural right thinking: that man as a creature of God is entitled to be treated with dignity and respect, that he has unalienable rights, and that government is instituted to secure these rights.

Today we are in the midst of a great social revolution. Old ideas, conventions, institutions, and restraints are challenged. A fierce new individualism with large claims to personal liberty is being asserted. The old morality seems to have been discredited, and a new permissiveness is dominant. A parallel and related development is a new egalitarianism, manifesting itself in the movement to end all discrimination based on race, color, religion, national ancestry, sex, age, and economic status. We are so close to these movements that we are likely to be blinded to their revolutionary and even radical character. A striking aspect is the legitimizing of these movements by constitutional interpretation. Constitutional thinking has been accommodated to the great movements of our day and in turn has contributed to them.

Despite the efforts of some justices to discredit the natural rights doctrine, it has recently reasserted itself in an interesting and dramatic way. In its significant 1965 decision in *Griswold* v. *Connecticut,* the Supreme Court reaffirmed a fundamental rights interpretation of due process of law by finding implicit in the concept of liberty a nation of personal privacy that includes the privacy of marriage and of the family relationship. Here the Court held invalid a Connecticut statute which forbade the use of contraceptives by married couples. The case presented some illuminating insights into the thinking of the justices.[29]

Mr. Justice Douglas—who shares with Justice Black an abhorrence of natural rights thinking because he associates it with the laissez-faire philosophy of earlier years—tried valiantly but not very persuasively to link the right of privacy, nowhere mentioned expressly in the Constitution, with the rights expressly stated in the Bill of Rights. Mr. Justice Goldberg dealt with the matter in a more forthright way. He recognized the rights pertaining to the marital estate, to home, and to family as fundamental in character and held that the Ninth Amendment to the Constitution permitted the courts to recognize and protect other rights besides those mentioned in the Bill of Rights—a proposition which of course has support in the long history of the fundamental rights interpretation of the Constitution. Justices Harlan and White similarly rested their case on the idea that the privacy of married life was a fundamental right which cannot be invaded except to serve a substantial public interest. Clearly a majority of the Court was reaching toward the idea of rights existing outside the Constitution.

Notwithstanding the dissent and Justice Douglas's protestations, *Griswold* v. *Connecticut* marked a significant revival of natural rights thinking, whatever the formal argument employed by the majority. It has been followed by recent cases—specifically, *Roe* v. *Wade* and *Doe* v. *Bolton*—where the Court has found that the liberty secured by the Fourteenth Amendment protects the right of a female to abort a foetus within the first six months of pregnancy. Our interest in this case here centers on the Court's use of a concept of right not explicit or even implicit in the

---

[29] See Kauper, "Penumbras, Peripheries, Emanations."

16

Constitution in order to strike down a state statute. Building on the right of privacy developed in *Griswold* v. *Connecticut,* the Court said that it was immaterial whether the right of privacy was derived from the fundamental rights interpretation of the due process clause or from the Ninth Amendment or from some peripheral aspect of a Bill of Rights guarantee. This decision strikingly affirms the classic notion that the liberty secured under the due process clause protects the so-called fundamental rights which the Court articulates by natural rights reasoning. These decisions have gone far to provide constitutional legitimacy for the current claims that a person has a constitutional freedom to the pursuit of happiness subject only to restrictions designed to protect compelling public interests. This is the Declaration of Independence all over again.

The vitality and persistence of fundamental rights thinking in the interpretation of the higher law is strikingly demonstrated in the interpretation of the equal protection clause. Despite early intimations that only the newly emancipated blacks would come within the protection of this clause, its special use to protect the black was virtually forgotten after the 1896 decision in *Plessy* v. *Ferguson* upholding the "separate but equal" doctrine. The great revitalization of equal protection came in 1954 in *Brown* v. *Board of Education* when the Court held that compulsory racial segregation in public schools resulted in unlawul discrimination against black children. Chief Justice Warren's opinion on the effect of segregation upon the life of the black child makes clear that legally imposed segregation could not be reconciled with the moral imperative underlying the equal protection idea. The Court was giving constitutional flesh and blood to the premise of the Declaration of Independence. But *Brown* v. *Board of Education* was only the beginning of a new chapter on equality.

Starting with the 1964 one-man one-vote decision of *Reynolds* v. *Sims,* the Court branched out in all directions in revitalizing the equal protection guarantee. In branching out, the Court has employed a new method of analysis. Classification must be subject to careful scrutiny by the Court if it rests on so-called suspect criteria or if the effect is to impair the enjoyment of a fundamental personal right. Discrimination falling into either of these two categories can be tolerated only if required by some compelling public interest. Thus discrimination based not only on race, color and religion, but on national ancestry, alien status, economic status, and illegitimacy of birth has been judicially condemned. The Supreme Court is now engaged in the process of accommodating the equal protection idea to the movement for liberation of the female sex from discrimination long sanctioned in law and practice.[30]

The movement in favor of equality is instructive for two reasons. First, it gives further constitutional sanction to that democratization of American life so well portrayed by Boorstin in his recent volume.[31] It also reflects an increasing awareness of the ethnic, racial, and religious diversity of America's pluralistic society. The new insistence on equality, which lays open to inquiry distinctions long tolerated in the law, and the new liberty, with its assertion of personal identity and freedom of expression, are responses to strong social currents of our day. Second, the revival in judicial opinions of the idea of fundamental right is a tribute to the persistence and vitality of natural rights thinking.

The intellectual process central to natural law thinking has a vitality of its own. It is indigenous to the judicial process under a written constitution. When the Court says that there must be a compelling public interest to warrant the restriction of a fundamental right or to justify discrimination resting on a suspect basis or impinging on a fundamental right, the Court is employing its own reasoning process to identify the right, to weigh the public interest, and to arrive at some accommodation. The higher law of the Constitution is thus embodied in the overriding judicial reasoning to which legislation is subject.

Why do some justices of the Court still feel obliged to file formal disclaimers against natural right thinking in the exposition

---

[30] For specific cases, see: national ancestry—Takahashi v. Fish & Game Commission, 334 U.S. 410 (1948) ; alien status—Graham v. Richardson, 403 U.S. 365 (1971) ; economic status—Douglas v. California, 372 U.S. 353 (1963), Harper v. Virginia Board of Elections, 383 U.S. 663 (1966), and Tate v. Short, 401 U.S. 395 (1971) ; illegitimacy—Levy v. Louisiana, 391 U.S. 68 (1968), and Weber v. Aetna Casualty & Surety Co., 406 U.S. 164 (1972) ; and women's rights—Reed v. Reed, 404 U.S. 71 (1971) ; Frontiero v. Richardson, 411 U.S. 677 (1973).

[31] Daniel J. Boorstin, *The Americans: The Democratic Experience* (New York: Random House, Inc., 1973).

of the Constitution? It is understandable that the general revulsion against ecclesiastical authority and the natural law associated with it, along with the decline in religious thinking that accompanied the new secularism in the last century, may have made the idea of natural right unpalatable to some. It is equally understandable that the idea of natural right became suspect when harnessed to support a laissez-faire philosophy. Yet it is true also that the whole doctrine of natural right, whether supported by religious or secular considerations, has had a long history in the thinking of the Western world. Rooted in antiquity, it was widely accepted at the time of the American Revolution, and the essential processes behind it have continued to be vital forces in constitutional interpretation. Indeed it is by constant recourse to these fundamental rights, however portrayed, that the Constitution has been accommodated to new strains of thought and new developments in our national life.

It is sometimes believed that natural right thinking is necessarily identified with a fixed body of dogma that defines natural rights so as to foreclose progressive application. This, of course, is not the case. Natural right thinking is dynamic, creative, and adaptable to new situations. As the late John Courtney Murray pointed out, the old idea of religious liberty limited to tolerance had its source in a different day and the new idea of religious liberty is a response to the new individual and social consciousness of our day.[32] It is also—one should add—a response to the pluralistic character of our society.

The argument is made, as Justice Black has made it, that unless the Court limits itself to the text of the Constitution it will become lost in subjective speculation. This, too, is a misconception. Natural right is not what any justice happens at the time to believe it ought to be. It is rather the result of rational discourse and dialogue based on the experience of the race and on fundamental philosophic and moral consideration regarding the nature of man and his relation to society. One need only look at the Universal Declaration of Human Rights adopted by the United

---

[32] J. C. Murray, *The Problem of Religious Freedom.*

Nations in 1948 [33] or at the preamble to the European Convention on Human Rights and Fundamental Freedoms of 1950 [34] to see that appeals to rights inhering in the dignity of the person and to the freedoms essential for a democratic society are still very much the mode and that the consensus reflected in these documents establishes an objective basis for the formulations of basic rights.

IV

We have a strong constitutional system. It has adapted itself to the extraordinary transformations in American political, economic, and social life, has both inspired and weathered silent and peaceable revolutions, and has created the condition of a free, open, and pluralistic society. The Founding Fathers built better than they knew. Asserting the right of revolution, they laid the foundation for a society that provides

---

[33] The U.N. declaration reads in part:

Whereas recognition of the inherent dignity and of the equal and inalienable rights of all members of the human family is the foundation of freedom, justice and peace in the world. [Preamble]

All human beings are born free and equal in dignity and rights. They are endowed with reason and conscience and should act towards one another in a spirit of brotherhood. [Article I]

For the text, see *Human Right: A Compilation of International Instruments of the United Nations* (New York: United Nations, 1967), p. 1.

[34] The preamble to the convention reads in part:

Considering the Universal Declaration of Human Rights proclaimed by the General Assembly of the United Nations on 10th December 1948; . . .

Reaffirming their profound belief in those Fundamental Freedoms which are the foundation of Justice and peace in the world and are best maintained on the one hand by an effective political democracy and on the other by a common understanding and observance of the Human Rights upon which they depend;

Being resolved, as the Governments of European countries which are likeminded and have a common heritage of political traditions, ideals, freedom and the rule of law to take the first steps for the collective enforcement of certain of the Rights stated in the Universal Declaration; . . .

For the text, see 213 United Nations Treaty Series 221 (1955).

peaceful means for growth and change. We have a system of judicial review which safeguards the integrity of our constitutional system and protects basic rights against abuse and the tyranny of the majority. Probably in no other democratic country are the freedoms for which the colonists were willing to sacrifice and die more fully protected. But, having grown accustomed to the constitutional protection of natural rights and having become self-indulgent in their enjoyment, we too easily forget that belief in natural rights helped spark the revolutionary movement. It is indeed good that we use the Bicentennial to refresh our appreciation of our freedoms and to capture again the excitement, daring, and devotion of the patriots who challenged authority when they threw the tea into Boston harbor, who responded to Paul Revere's midnight ride with the confrontations at Lexington and Concord.

This is not to say that all is well with the system. I suggested earlier that the idea of right is not static and that part of our current problem is to address the idea of right to our current needs. In this day of sophisticated electronic surveillance and data storage and retrieval, the newly formulated right of privacy requires recognition and implementation. At a time of proliferating regulation in a complex urban society, the liberty of the individual to maintain some degree of identity and to pursue a path of self-respect requires us to be skeptical of a paternalism whereby Big Brother peeks over the citizen's shoulder to tell him what is good for him. The unrestrained exploitation of our resources and the debasement of the environment require a recognition that all citizens together have a natural right to enjoy their common resources and environment, a right more compelling than the freedom once claimed in the name of laissez-faire to plunder resources, pollute the air, and impair the amenities of living. The rights of all citizens regardless of race or color to equal opportunity for achievement, free from the blight of discrimination, are still only imperfectly realized. Equally important is the realization that the classic idea of natural right as restraint on government, so well captured in our system, is no longer adequate to the needs of a society where substantial pockets of poverty, hunger, disadvantage and want persist, notwithstanding the general state of affluence. Indeed, for those trapped in the web of our system, the responsibility of society to meet basic economic and social needs may be more significant than the traditional restraints designed to protect liberty against the abuse of power.

Equally important in this day of heightened international concern, a day marked by the tide of rising expectations of the have-not peoples, is a recognition that their rights and freedoms are inextricably entwined with ours. We can no longer indulge in a parochial view of our rights and interests, ignoring the responsibility for sharing our resources with others and for supporting their aspirations to the freedoms and satisfactions we claim for ourselves. The Declaration of Human Rights adopted by the United Nations, a declaration to which the United States is a party, is a ringing affirmation of the great words that *"all* men are created equal and endowed by their creator with certain unalienable rights."[35]

More troubling are symptoms of an uneasiness in American thought and life as we approach the nation's bicentennial and contemplate the nation's future. Pessimism and cynicism are widespread. Power has been shamefully abused by men who have wielded it free from a sense of moral or political responsibility. Illegal tactics directed to winning elections are an ugly blow at the integrity of the political process. The trustworthiness and credibility of the people's servants have been deeply eroded, with a resulting loss of faith in the whole political process. Extravagant campaign expenditures, financed by large contributions from those who have special interests to protect, undermine the freedom of elected representatives to serve the public interest. Freedom of the press too often becomes an excuse for distortion and manipulation of news, invasion of privacy, and intrusions into those judicial processes designed to maintain the conditions of a fair hearing for those charged with wrongdoing. Private groups—business, labor, interests of all kinds—are bastions of power which sometimes rival the government in the authority they exercise. The new freedom characterized by the sloughing off of old moral restraints finds expression in license and permissiveness. The new egalitarianism risks cheapening American life and culture and eroding the sense of excellence. The pursuit of materialistic gratifications, also claimed in the name of liberty, has dulled the conscience and

---

[35] Emphasis supplied.

22

impaired our vision of the enduring spiritual values that make a people great.

And so it appears to many that the spark ignited by the American Revolution, the vitality and lively expectations which guided the Founding Fathers, have been dimmed and corroded by selfishness, corruption, and anomie.

But we need not despair. Indeed, a healthful pessimism underlies the idea of a government of limited powers and the rule of law—the recognition of the evil in man and the need for restraints to check his abuse of power. Power does corrupt. This in itself is a basic premise of natural law and one which underlies our system. The basic checks and balances of our system are even more essential to the maintenance of freedom than the rights formally declared in the Constitution. The very fact that flagrant abuse of power has been uncovered and that the Congress is now reasserting its authority against extravagant claims of executive authority is itself evidence of the strength and resiliency of our system.

We have the means of curbing large concentrations of power, whether in the public or private sectors, if only we have the understanding and determination to do so. But, even more important, we have the resources of mind and spirit needed to cleanse our society of its grossness, its preoccupation with material ends—to recapture the dedication and fire which inspired the Revolution in order to inspire the revitalization of today's society.

The pessimism that is an important ingredient of our constitutional thinking is balanced by an optimism—a faith that men can work together to achieve common goals in a society held together by a sense of civil righteousness. This is the faith we must again cultivate. But later generations cannot endlessly harvest fruit from the trees others have planted and cultivated. There must be in our day a restoration of faith in the basic institutions that have served us so well and that constitute what Walter Lippmann has called the public philosophy. There must be continued vigilance in the nurture of ideas and institutions which are our higher law heritage. There must be renewed appreciation of our heritage of rights and freedoms and renewed insistence on the premises underlying the conception of natural right. There must be a restoration of integrity in the affairs of government, decency in public life, and civility and reasoned discourse in the great debate on issues of public concern. There must be sensitivity, compassion, and generosity in response to human needs. There must be self-restraint and responsibility in the exercise of freedom, lest freedom degenerate into licentiousness and anarchy. There must be an affirmation of the moral values which undergird the public order. There must be an assessment of our rights and liberties as more than negative restraints, as positive means for self-development and service to others. Freedom without purpose, discipline, and regard for the common good is self-destroying.

I have suggested that, in the end, the institutions we deem important and the significance of the rights we assert must rest upon some consensus in the public mind about the values we hold —upon the content of the contemporary natural law. I have further suggested that this consensus depends upon shared moral perceptions and understanding. Whether a nation can long survive without substantial consensus on overriding values is a question which invites serious discussion. There was a time when it could be said that we were a Christian nation, guided in regard to national values by the Christian ethic. That time is past. In our pluralistic society with its diverse religious elements no single religion can claim for itself a favored position in the law, and the law in turn may not reflect the views of a single religious community.

Where, if at all, can a basis be found for the moral consensus which is the heart of natural law? Historical tradition is important. The accepted views of nations are relevant. To others it may appear that the Constitution and the values it embodies constitute our moral consensus and that the Supreme Court serves the function of moulding and interpreting our higher law. But as I have stressed before, dangers lurk in the view that ultimate ideas of wisdom, justice and morality are embodied in a written legal instrument. The ultimate ideas and the transcendent values must, in their very nature, lie outside the Constitution, just as basic rights have their source outside the Constitution. It is a form of idol worship to see the Constitution as the expression of ultimate values in our nation's life.

Moreover, it is dangerous to rely on an institution—more particularly a tribunal of nine men—for the ultimate exposition of our national values. It is sometimes said that the Supreme Court is the conscience of the nation. This is specious. The Court cannot impose its notion of conscience without regard to the accepted moral values of the community. It can lead, but within limits. In the end its decision on ultimate values must be sustained by some higher law rooted in the common consciousness and understanding.

The current revolution, centering on the new freedoms and making extraordinary claims in the name of personal liberty, raises questions about the limits of this liberty and the organ responsible for determining these limits. While natural law supports a theory of natural rights, it also asserts man's social obligations so that one man's rights are limited by the rights of others and by important social interests, including those moral values which are rooted in the conscience and traditions of the people. Moreover, the legislative branch too has a voice in expressing the people's moral concern, and its expression of that concern should not be lightly disregarded by the courts. The abortion cases reflect the danger of having the Supreme Court assume the role, at the expense of the Congress, as the nation's conscience in determining important questions of public policy.

The conscience of the nation lies outside the Constitution and supports it. The beliefs rooted in common understanding are the stuff of a nation's aspiration and moral vision. Our hope of giving contemporary meaning to the higher law and the natural rights of man lies in the shaping of a common ethic which draws its inspiration from religious, moral, and philosophical sources, which is illuminated by history, fortified by the ringing affirmation of the great Declaration, and given concrete application through the reasoned discourse which is the hallmark of a great society.